JOHN IS A FATHER

Julie Marie Myatt

BROADWAY PLAY PUBLISHING INC
New York
www.broadwayplaypublishing.com
info@broadwayplaypublishing.com

JOHN IS A FATHER
© Copyright 2019 Julie Marie Myatt

Cover photo: Julie Marie Myatt

First edition: August 2019
I S B N: 978-0-88145-815-2

Book design: Marie Donovan
Page make-up: Adobe InDesign
Typeface: Palatino

JOHN IS A FATHER was first produced at The Road Theatre Company (Producers, Donna Simone Johnson and Ann Hearn) in North Hollywood, running from 3 May–16 July 2016. The cast and creative contributors were:

JOHN OWENS	Sam Anderson
EDWARD	Mark Costello
KENNETH	Carl J Johnson
DOUG	John Gowans
PATRICIA	Hilary J Schwartz
REGGIE	Jackson Dollinger & Elliot Decker

Director	Dan Bonnell
Set design	Tom Buderwitz
Lighting & projection design	Tom Ontiveros
Sound design	David Marling
Costume design	Michele Young
Stage manager	Maurie Gonzalez

The play was nominated for a 2016 L A Stage Alliance Ovation Award for Playwriting of an Original Play.

NOTE ON MUSIC

For performance of copyrighted songs, arrangements or recordings referenced in this play, permission of the copyright owner(s) must be obtained. Other songs, arrangements or recordings may be substituted provided permission from the copyright owner(s) of such songs, arrangements or recordings is obtained or songs, arrangements or recordings in the public domain may be substituted.

CHARACTERS & SETTING

EDWARD
JOHN OWENS
KENNETH
DOUG
PATRICIA
REGGIE

Time: 2014

Place: A city sidewalk, Los Angeles
An apartment
An airport food court
A motel room
An apartment, Phoenix

Suggested music: Merle Haggard, Johnny Cash—songs of
the past

Scene 1

(A city sidewalk, Los Angeles)

(A man in his early seventies, JOHN OWENS, *wears an old straw cowboy hat, old cowboy boots, and carries a small bag of groceries. He has a slow gait—somewhere between a cowboy and a plumber. Legs slightly bowed, slightly aching. He's in no hurry to get anywhere.)*

*(*EDWARD, *an old homeless man in his late seventies, sits by his over-stuffed shopping cart taking a nap. His mouth wide open.)*

*(*JOHN *stops beside* EDWARD.*)*

JOHN: Hey there.

(Silence)

*(*JOHN *looks closer.)*

JOHN: Edward?

*(*EDWARD *keeps sleeping.)*

*(*JOHN *taps his arm with his boot.)*

JOHN: You alive?
(He taps him again with his boot.)
Edward.

*(*EDWARD *slowly wakes.)*

(Silence)

*(*EDWARD *just looks at* JOHN.*)*

EDWARD: What's it look like?

JOHN: Hard to tell.

EDWARD: I'm talking to you, aren't I.

JOHN: Well. Okay. That's good.

(Silence)

EDWARD: Maybe. I don't know.

JOHN: Anyone ever come and try and carry you off?

EDWARD: When?

JOHN: When you're sleeping?

EDWARD: Like who?

JOHN: The city.

EDWARD: Oh. Yes. Plenty.

JOHN: You have a real dead look when you sleep.

EDWARD: So I've been told.
(He adjusts himself. Rubs his face with his hand)
A man has to sleep.

JOHN: Yes.

EDWARD: I can't control how I look when I'm sleeping.

JOHN: I guess not.

EDWARD: I'm just…sleeping. Out of my control. How I look.

JOHN: Sure.

EDWARD: I don't know why everyone gets all hot about things.

JOHN: I'm not hot.

EDWARD: Geez. A man's gotta be himself. Doesn't he?

JOHN: I'm just observing.

EDWARD: You and everyone else.

(JOHN pulls bananas and apples out of his bag and hands them to EDWARD.)

EDWARD: That's four bananas. And six apples.

JOHN: Yeah.

EDWARD: You usually give me three. And two apples—

JOHN: They were on sale, so I thought I'd get—

EDWARD: I can't eat four bananas. No. No.

JOHN: Why not?

EDWARD: Three's my limit.

JOHN: What do you want me to do with it?

EDWARD: Take it home.

JOHN: No.

EDWARD: Take it.

JOHN: I don't eat bananas.

EDWARD: What's wrong with you?

JOHN: I won't be in town.

EDWARD: Why?

JOHN: I'm—

EDWARD: I'll keep it. Geez. I don't like this, but I'll keep it.

JOHN: I know you have your system.

EDWARD: I'm just used to three bananas and two apples a day. That's all.
(He puts the fruit beside him.)
Thank you.

JOHN: You're welcome.

EDWARD: I hope they don't rot.

JOHN: I'm going to be—

EDWARD: That'll be on you. If they do.

JOHN: I'm going to be gone for a bit.

EDWARD: What?

JOHN: I'm just going to be gone. For a little while.

EDWARD: Where?

JOHN: I'm taking a trip.

EDWARD: A trip. Why?

(*Silence*)

JOHN: I'm going to meet my grandson.

EDWARD: You have a grandson?

JOHN: Yes.

EDWARD: No kidding.

JOHN: No—

EDWARD: I didn't know you had family.

JOHN: Well. I do.

EDWARD: What do you got? A son? Daughter? Both?

JOHN: A son.

EDWARD: Where's your wife?

JOHN: Texas.

EDWARD: Why Texas? Divorced?

JOHN: Yes.

EDWARD: I don't like Texas. Never have liked it.

JOHN: Okay.

EDWARD: Then where's your grandson?

JOHN: Phoenix.

EDWARD: Phoenix. So that's where you're going?

JOHN: Yes.

EDWARD: Jesus.

(*Silence*)

Phoenix. I went there once. Hot. Dry. A lot of golf.

JOHN: Huh.

EDWARD: That's what I remember. You play?

JOHN: No.

EDWARD: What?

JOHN: I don't play golf.

EDWARD: I played once. Kind of boring if ask me.

JOHN: Seems so.

EDWARD: Chasing a ball for five hours.

JOHN: Seems long.

EDWARD: I went to Phoenix when I got out of the Marine Corps.

JOHN: My son was a Marine.

EDWARD: Once a Marine, always a Marine.

JOHN: That's what they say.

EDWARD: It's true. You?

JOHN: Marine? No. No.

EDWARD: Army?

JOHN: No.

EDWARD: Air Force?

JOHN: No.

EDWARD: Navy?

JOHN: No.

EDWARD: You dodge the draft?

JOHN: Something like that.

(Silence)

(More silence)

(EDWARD stares at JOHN.)

JOHN: Are you upset with me now?

EDWARD: I don't know.
(*Silence*)
Maybe.

JOHN: That was a long time ago.

EDWARD: Yes and no.
(*Silence*)
I don't like draft dodgers.
(*Silence*)

JOHN: I was in prison, Edward.

EDWARD: Prison?

JOHN: Yes.

EDWARD: What for?

JOHN: It's not important.

EDWARD: You kill someone?

JOHN: No.

EDWARD: What?

JOHN: No. I didn't.
(*Silence*)

EDWARD: Well, I was in Vietnam. I didn't dodge.

JOHN: I know that. I remember that.

EDWARD: How?

JOHN: You told me once. Or twice.
(*Silence*)

EDWARD: I loved being a Marine. Straightened me right up.

JOHN: Uh huh.

EDWARD: Probably would have done you some good.

JOHN: Maybe.

EDWARD: It would have.

(Silence)
I killed people, you know.

JOHN: Yes.

EDWARD: I had to. We all had to. I regret that.

JOHN: I'm sure you do.

(Silence)

EDWARD: That's just what we had to do.

JOHN: Yes.

EDWARD: That's war.

JOHN: Yes it is.

EDWARD: No one likes it.
(Silence)
It's war not a picnic.

JOHN: Yes.
(Silence)
I should get home—

EDWARD: I was married once too, you know. But she died.

JOHN: You told me that.

EDWARD: I did?

JOHN: Yes.

EDWARD: We never had children.

(Silence)

JOHN: Did you want them?

EDWARD: Yes.

JOHN: Sorry to hear that.

EDWARD: We wanted them pretty bad. What can you do?

JOHN: I don't know.

EDWARD: Keep on going on, I guess. Just go on.

JOHN: Yes.

EDWARD: That's life.

JOHN: I guess so.

(Silence)

EDWARD: When are you coming back?

JOHN: Sunday.

EDWARD: You driving?

JOHN: Flying.

EDWARD: Isn't that expensive?

JOHN: A bit.

EDWARD: How'd you pay for it?

JOHN: What do you mean, how'd I pay for it?

EDWARD: How'd you pay for it? Are you rich?

(Silence)

JOHN: With credit.

EDWARD: Credit? Are you crazy?

JOHN: No—

EDWARD: You better not get in debt.

JOHN: Don't you worry about me.

EDWARD: That's a sink hole. That debt. Don't get me started on that.

JOHN: I won't.

EDWARD: Starts with one plane ticket, and the next thing you know, you're selling the house, they're taking back the car, and the dog has to go live with the neighbors.

JOHN: I'll be fine.

EDWARD: A good dog too.

JOHN: Uh huh.

EDWARD: It's awful, that debt.

JOHN: I'll be fine, Edward. Don't worry.

EDWARD: You better.
(Silence)
Watch yourself.

JOHN: I will.

EDWARD: I haven't been on a plane in twenty years.

JOHN: Well, it's been awhile for me. I don't know how long—

EDWARD: I hear they don't feed you anymore.

JOHN: Yeah.

(Silence)

EDWARD: How long you going for?

JOHN: A few days.

EDWARD: What?

JOHN: A few days.

EDWARD: What day you coming back?

JOHN: Sunday.

EDWARD: Sunday evening or morning?

JOHN: Evening.

EDWARD: So I won't see you until Monday.

JOHN: Probably not.

EDWARD: Don't go using that credit willy-nilly while you're there.

JOHN: Okay.

EDWARD: I mean it.

JOHN: I know you do.

EDWARD: I guess I'll see you Monday.

JOHN: Monday it is.

EDWARD: You nervous?

JOHN: About what?

EDWARD: Flying?

JOHN: No.

EDWARD: I used to get nervous. After Vietnam. I used to get real nervous on planes.

JOHN: Yeah?

EDWARD: Yeah. Couldn't tell you why. Not directly.

(JOHN checks his watch.)

EDWARD: I'll let you go.

JOHN: Okay.

EDWARD: You in a hurry?

JOHN: No.

EDWARD: Why you checking your watch?

JOHN: I have things to do.

EDWARD: Then I'll let you go.

JOHN: Okay.

EDWARD: Oh, can you bring me something from that plane?

JOHN: Like what?

EDWARD: I don't know. A souvenir of some sort.

JOHN: Like what?

EDWARD: A napkin or something.

JOHN: Sure.

EDWARD: Or a cup. A cup. You decide.

JOHN: Okay.

EDWARD: Be creative.

JOHN: I'll see what I can do.

EDWARD: Thanks.
(Silence)
You're coming back, right?

JOHN: Yes.

EDWARD: Don't forget my souvenir from the plane,
Okay?

JOHN: Okay.

EDWARD: Okay then. Be careful.

JOHN: I will.

(EDWARD closes his eyes, goes back to sleep.)

(End of conversation)

(JOHN keeps walking.)

Scene 2

*(JOHN packs his small, old suitcase. He folds each shirt
carefully.)*

(He folds a pair of pants.)

(He carefully folds a jacket.)

(He is exacting in his packing.)

(Socks. Underwear)

(This is a process.)

(He adds another pair of socks.)

(His dopp kit)

*(A present, awkwardly wrapped in bright blue paper, sits
beside him.)*

(He puts that in last. Careful not to mess it up)

(He looks around to see if there's anything he's forgotten.)

(Stands thinking. Anything else?)

(He closes the suitcase. Snaps it)

(He puts it on the floor.)

(He looks at his boot. Sees a spot, and uses a bit of spit to get it off.)

(He puts on his hat.)

(Picks up the suitcase, and looks himself in the mirror)

(Ready?)

(No. Not yet)

(He sets down the suitcase.)

(Looks around the room)

(Time to give it one more try)

(He picks up the suit case again.)

Scene 3

(Airport fast-food area.)

(JOHN holds a bag of fast food, and a cup of coffee, and his suitcase. It's awkward, trying to hold it all.)

(He finds an empty table.)

(He sits down and catches his breath. He takes a sip of coffee. It's hot. He slowly unwraps his hamburger.)

(A couple, KENNETH and DOUG enter with roller bags and trays of food, searching for a place to sit.)

(The only seats available are next to JOHN.)

KENNETH: Sir? I'm, I'm sorry, do you mind? There's no other place to sit, and we—

JOHN: No. Please. Go ahead. I don't mind.

KENNETH: Thank you.

DOUG: Thank you.

KENNETH: They really should have more places to sit.

DOUG: They should.

JOHN: Oh?
(He looks around.)
Yes. Probably.

DOUG: They're probably trying to save money.
Someone's always trying to save money, somewhere.
Somehow.

KENNETH: Where's my bag, Doug?

DOUG: You're holding it.

KENNETH: Good. Good. Right. You have your wallet?

DOUG: Yes.

KENNETH: Our boarding passes? You didn't lose them
did you?

DOUG: No.

KENNETH: Let me see them.

DOUG: They're in my briefcase.

KENNETH: You're sure?

DOUG: Yes.

(DOUG and KENNETH settle in.)

KENNETH: It's so stressful to travel.

DOUG: It really is.

JOHN: Yes.

KENNETH: It just makes me anxious, I guess.

DOUG: I know it does.

KENNETH: I can't help it.

DOUG: I know.

(KENNETH *takes a big breath.*)

(*He smiles at* JOHN.)

KENNETH: I like your hat.

JOHN: Oh. Thank you. (*Silence*) I forgot I had it on. (*He takes it off, and looks for a place to put it. Settles on place it on tope of his suitcase. Adjusts his hair. And continues to eat.*)

KENNETH: Where are you going?

(KENNETH *catches* JOHN *mid-bite.*)

DOUG: Let him eat, Kenneth.

KENNETH: I'm sorry. I don't want to bother you. Keep eating. You should eat.
(*He waits.*)

DOUG: He's kind of a nervous talker.

KENNETH: It's the travel.

DOUG: I know.

(JOHN *swallows.*)

KENNETH: I can't help it.

JOHN: Phoenix.

KENNETH: Oh, Phoenix. Arizona. Lovely. Hot. It's a dry heat.

DOUG: Lots of golf there.

JOHN: That's what I hear.

KENNETH: We're going to Seattle. Doug has family there.

DOUG: It's a wedding.

JOHN: Nice.

DOUG: Well.

(*Silence*)

KENNETH: What's in Phoenix? You from there?

JOHN: No.

KENNETH: You have family there?

JOHN: My grandson.

KENNETH: Wonderful. A grandson. How old?

JOHN: Seven. I think.
(He thinks, counting in his head.)

JOHN: Yes, must be about seven now.

(Silence)

KENNETH: Seven. Good age.

JOHN: Is it? I hope so.

KENNETH: You haven't you met him before.

DOUG: Kenneth—

KENNETH: What?

JOHN: No.

DOUG: We don't mean to intrude.

KENNETH: Well, then this is a big trip for you.

(Silence)

JOHN: Yes it is.

KENNETH: I'm sure he's excited to meet you.

JOHN: Maybe. We'll see.

KENNETH: Doug just loved his grandfather.

DOUG: More than my father, actually.

KENNETH: No one likes your father.

DOUG: True.

KENNETH: *(To* JOHN*)* He's awful.

DOUG: Pretty much.

KENNETH: I really don't know how Doug did it. Growing up with him. Mine left when I was two, so you know…

DOUG: Now's not the time.

KENNETH: What's his name?

JOHN: Who?

KENNETH: Your grandson.

JOHN: Oh. Uh. Reggie. After his grandpa, I think. His, his other grandpa.

KENNETH: Is it your daughter or son's…?

DOUG: Kenneth.

JOHN: My son.

KENNETH: Wonderful. Your son.

JOHN: Yes.

KENNETH: You must be excited to see him.

JOHN: He was killed. In Afghanistan.

(Silence)

KENNETH: Oh.

DOUG: I'm, I'm sorry to hear that.

KENNETH: I'm sorry—

DOUG: I hope we aren't making you uncomfortable.

JOHN: No. No.

KENNETH: Gosh.

DOUG: I am sorry.

KENNETH: What was his name?

JOHN: Henry.

KENNETH: I've always liked that name. Haven't I, Doug?

DOUG: Yes.

KENNETH: Henry.

JOHN: Henry Owens.
(*Silence*)
That was my father's name.

KENNETH: Great, great name. Uh huh. Henry Owens.
(*Silence*)
I am sorry.

DOUG: Yes.

JOHN: I didn't want him to join the Marines, but…

DOUG: Sure.

KENNETH: I'm very anti-military. Frankly. Very.

(*Silence*)

JOHN: Kids want to do what they want to do.

KENNETH: I guess.

DOUG: Yes.

KENNETH: Doug grew his hair. Down to his waist.

DOUG: Well.

KENNETH: You should have seen it. He looked like Cher.

DOUG: No.

KENNETH: That's what your father said.

DOUG: Well.

KENNETH: He cut it off before I met him.

DOUG: It was a lot of maintenance. That hair.
(*Silence*)

JOHN: I'm keeping you folks from eating.

DOUG: No, no.

(*Silence*)

KENNETH: I'm always too nervous to eat before I fly anyway. Really. We'll probably have to pack this up.

DOUG: That's true.

KENNETH: I really don't like flying. I hate it, actually.

DOUG: He has to take a Xanax.
(He checks his watch.)
You should take it in about ten minutes, honey.

KENNETH: Thanks.

JOHN: I'm not too crazy about flying either.

KENNETH: You want a Xanax?

JOHN: No thank you.

KENNETH: I have plenty.

JOHN: I'll just white-knuckle it.
(He smiles, takes a drink from his coffee.)

(Silence)

JOHN: This coffee is pretty good.

KENNETH: Is Henry's wife picking you up?

JOHN: I'm sorry?

KENNETH: Your grandson's mother? Is she meeting you at the airport?

DOUG: Kenneth.

KENNETH: What?

DOUG: I'm sorry. He can be…I'm Doug. This is Kenneth. By the way.
(He puts out his hand.)

JOHN: John. Owens.

DOUG: Nice to meet you.

KENNETH: I'm really not trying to pry.

DOUG: He's naturally nosey.

KENNETH: I call it curious.

DOUG: I know you do.

JOHN: Henry and I weren't on good terms.

KENNETH: I see. That's too bad. I've never had children, but I can imagine that is very hard.

JOHN: Yes.

(Silence)

KENNETH: We have two dogs. But you can't compare, right?

JOHN: No.

DOUG: He treats them like kids.

KENNETH: And you don't?

DOUG: Well.

(Silence)

KENNETH: Your son's wife is picking you up? At the airport?

JOHN: No. I've never met her. She sounds nice on the telephone. As much as you can tell.

KENNETH: You didn't meet her at his funeral?

DOUG: (Kenneth. Really.)

KENNETH: (What?)

JOHN: No.

KENNETH: Why not?

DOUG: (Kenneth.)

JOHN: I wasn't invited.

KENNETH: What? He was your son.

(Silence)

JOHN: When he was young. I…
(Silence)

I deserved it, I guess.

(*Silence*)

KENNETH: No one deserves not to be there to bury his own son.

(*Silence*)

(JOHN *wraps up his hamburger.*)

(DOUG *touches* KENNETH's *hand.*)

(*He glances at him.*)

(JOHN *drinks his coffee.*)

(*Silence*)

KENNETH: It's, it's nice his wife invited you to come visit.

JOHN: Yes.

(*Silence*)

I think so.

DOUG: This is a big trip for you.

KENNETH: Are you nervous? I would be. I'd be scared to death.

JOHN: I'm not much of a traveler.

KENNETH: I get very nervous. Like I said. About most things. Frankly.

DOUG: As you can tell.

KENNETH: Doug.

DOUG: Well.

(*Silence*)

KENNETH: Do you have any plans? While you're there?

JOHN: With my grandson?

KENNETH: Yes.

JOHN: I hadn't really thought that far ahead. Tell you the truth.

DOUG: Of course not. Kenneth is a planner. To the maximum.

KENNETH: I can't help it. I like a schedule. I like to know what I'm going to do.

JOHN: I'm more of a go with the flow.

DOUG: Me too.

KENNETH: Douglas.

DOUG: Left to my own devices, I would be.

KENNETH: Well, that's why you have me. Your "devices" would never get anything done, honey. Not on time.

DOUG: Probably true.

KENNETH: He's a procrastinator.

DOUG: Guilty.

JOHN: Some of us take longer to do things.

DOUG: Exactly.

KENNETH: Or wait until someone else does them. Or we get nagged to death until we finally do.

DOUG: Uh huh.

KENNETH: True.

DOUG: Well.

(Silence)

KENNETH: Do you have a place to stay in Phoenix? Are you staying in a hotel?

DOUG: Though it's really none of our business.

KENNETH: It's a simple question.

JOHN: I found a Motel Six near by.

KENNETH: That's good.

JOHN: Should be fine. It's got a pretty good rate.

DOUG: That helps.

KENNETH: Sure.

DOUG: Don't forget to ask for a senior discount.

KENNETH: Doug is the king of the senior discount.

DOUG: You have to ask for it. They won't just give it you automatically.

JOHN: Okay.

(Silence)

KENNETH: I can't imagine how you feel.

(Silence)

(JOHN *sips his coffee. He looks around.*)

KENNETH: What are you looking for? What do you need?

JOHN: Napkin.

KENNETH: Here.

(KENNETH *hands* JOHN *a stack from his tray.*)

KENNETH: I have plenty.

JOHN: Thank you.

(DOUG *looks at his food.*)

(Silence)

KENNETH: I was very against the war. Frankly. I'm sorry. I'll admit it. I still am.

DOUG: Kenneth.

JOHN: Well. Me too.

KENNETH: But that doesn't mean I don't respect what your son sacrificed. Really. I mean that. Sincerely.

JOHN: Yes.

KENNETH: But it all seems a waste to me. A terrible terrible waste. Of life. For what? For what?

(*Silence*)

JOHN: Well.

(*Silence*)

DOUG: (Honey.)

KENNETH: Do you have other children?

JOHN: No.

KENNETH: Your only son?

JOHN: Yes. That I know of.

(*Silence*)

KENNETH: See, Doug? His only son. His only son.

DOUG: Okay—

KENNETH: For what? They don't even like us in Afghanistan.

DOUG: No one likes us, Kenneth. Not anymore.

KENNETH: And who could blame them?

DOUG: I know.

KENNETH: It's awful. I'm embarrassed to be an American. Most days. Aren't you?

JOHN: No.

KENNETH: Really?

JOHN: You can't please everyone.

DOUG: That is true. I agree with you there.

KENNETH: I'd like to please some people.

DOUG: It's all about money.

KENNETH: Maybe.

DOUG: It is, honey. It is all about money. Or oil.

KENNETH: It's disgusting.

DOUG: Money or oil or pride. Or power. Somewhere. Somehow. It's about something else.

KENNETH: I'm tired of it.

DOUG: Well.

(Silence)

JOHN: You all have barely touched your food.

DOUG: It's not very good.

KENNETH: It's horrible.

DOUG: Well.

KENNETH: We should just pack it up. Don't you think, honey?

DOUG: Will we eat it later?

KENNETH: Probably not.

DOUG: I hate to leave it.

(Silence)

JOHN: Seems like a waste.

DOUG: It does.

KENNETH: I'm too nervous to eat. I don't know why I try.

DOUG: You have to try.

KENNETH: I know.

DOUG: They won't serve anything on the plane.

KENNETH: It's a short trip.

DOUG: Still.

KENNETH: I'm really not hungry. I don't even know what this is.

DOUG: Chicken.

KENNETH: Is it?

DOUG: I'll wrap it up. Just in case.
(*He wraps up the food.*)
We paid an arm and a leg for it.

JOHN: Prices are high here.

DOUG: They really are. Airports. They know they've got you where they want you.

(*Silence*)

KENNETH: What time is your flight?

JOHN: Pardon?

KENNETH: What time is your—

JOHN: Oh. Four o'clock.

KENNETH: You're early.

(JOHN *checks his watch.*)

JOHN: I guess I am.

KENNETH: I like to be early too. I mean, why rush and make yourself crazy.

JOHN: Sure.

DOUG: He's been up since five.

KENNETH: I can't help it.

JOHN: Sure.

KENNETH: You have a magazine for the plane? Or a book?

JOHN: No. I don't think I do.

KENNETH: I have extra. I can give you one of mine. Doug, hand me my bag.

DOUG: You're still wearing it.

KENNETH: Goodness.
(*He digs out a stack of magazines.*)

DOUG: He might want to sleep on the plane.

KENNETH: Well, I'm never going to read all these.
(*He holds out the options.*)
Any of these interest you? *People*? *Time*? *Martha Stewart*?

JOHN: That's alright.

KENNETH: Really. Our flight's not that long. And the Xanax usually knocks me out. Frankly. And look at this? You'd think I was going all the way to China. *New Yorker*? *Us*?

JOHN: What about Doug?

DOUG: I have a book. I'm not much of a magazine guy.

JOHN: Oh.

DOUG: History buff.

KENNETH: See? Take one. It'll make the time go faster. I can't imagine you're much of a Martha Stewart fan.

JOHN: No.

KENNETH: Not looking for new recipes?

JOHN: Not right now.

KENNETH: I really just look at the pictures myself. Who has five hours these days to spend making an apple pie? I have a job, for Christ's sake.

DOUG: Time is the next crisis.

KENNETH: *Time* magazine?

DOUG: No. Literal time. We're all running out of it. Time. No one has enough time.

(*Silence*)

KENNETH: I don't understand.

DOUG: I mean no one has enough time anymore—

KENNETH: Sometimes you are a little too deep or obscure for me, Doug. I don't know which.

DOUG: I'll explain later.

(KENNETH *turns her attention back to* JOHN.)

KENNETH: How about *People*?
(*He shows the cover of* People.)
People's really just celebrity gossip. With pictures.

JOHN: Looks like it.

KENNETH: My guilty pleasure.

JOHN: You keep it.

KENNETH: Okay. How about *Time*?
(*To* DOUG)
The magazine.

DOUG: I'll explain later.

JOHN: I used to have a subscription to *Time*. It's been years—

KENNETH: It's yours.

JOHN: No.

KENNETH: Please. That settles it.

JOHN: Are you sure?

(KENNETH *hands it to* JOHN.)

KENNETH: It will lighten my bag. Really.

JOHN: Not by much.

KENNETH: I'll take it.

DOUG: He's carrying the kitchen sink in there.

KENNETH: He exaggerates.

DOUG: Only slightly.

KENNETH: True. Frankly.

JOHN: Well. Thank you. I appreciate that.

KENNETH: I think there's some good articles in there.

JOHN: I'll look forward to it.

(He smiles at him.)

(KENNETH *looks at his watch.*)

KENNETH: I think we should probably go to our gate, Doug. Just to make sure we know where it is. I don't want us to go the wrong way.

DOUG: Okay.

KENNETH: It was very nice to meet you, John.

JOHN: Yes. You too. You too.

KENNETH: I hope you have a great trip. We'll be thinking of you. Won't we, Doug?

DOUG: Yes. He literally will. I promise you.

KENNETH: I can't help it.
(He takes a chocolate bar out of his bag.)

KENNETH: Here.

JOHN: Oh—

KENNETH: I always carry chocolate. My niece thinks I'm the best person in the world because of it.

DOUG: He spoils her.

KENNETH: She's seven too.

JOHN: Is she?

KENNETH: Great age. We imagine a lot of things together.

DOUG: Kenneth has her designing kingdoms and building castles for hours.

KENNETH: We drink a lot of tea and a kill a lot of dragons.

DOUG: She wears him out.

KENNETH: You've got to get down on their level. Literally. Right down there on the floor.

(JOHN *nods.*)

KENNETH: But I'm a kid at heart, I guess.

DOUG: He is.

(KENNETH *pushes the chocolate towards* JOHN.)

JOHN: Thank you.

KENNETH: My pleasure.
(*He remembers. Points at the chocolate*)
There's no nuts in that either. In case he has allergies.

(*Silence*)

DOUG: Ready, sweetheart?

KENNETH: You have our boarding passes?

DOUG: Yes.

KENNETH: Let me see them.

DOUG: They're in my briefcase. I'm not digging them out—

KENNETH: Okay, okay. My Xanax? Doug. Shoot. I forgot to—

DOUG: I'll give it to you at the gate.

KENNETH: Okay, okay. Fine. Good idea.

(DOUG *and* KENNETH *stand.*)

(KENNETH *puts out his hand.*)

KENNETH: So nice to meet you.

(JOHN *takes it.*)

KENNETH: I hope it's a great great trip.

JOHN: Thank you. You too.

(KENNETH *finally lets go of* JOHN'*s hand.*)

DOUG: Nice to meet you, John.

(DOUG *puts out his hand.* JOHN *takes it.*)

JOHN: Thank you. Enjoy the wedding.

DOUG: Well.

KENNETH: Don't forget to drink water on the plane. It's easy to get dehydrated and not even know it.

JOHN: Thank you.

KENNETH: And when you're in Phoenix too. It's dry there. You need to stay hydrated.

JOHN: I appreciate that.

DOUG: What did I tell you? He'll be thinking about you.

KENNETH: I will.
(*He touches* JOHN's *shoulder.*)
Okay. Bye now.

JOHN: Goodbye.

KENNETH: Take care of yourself.

DOUG: Safe travels.

JOHN: Thank you. You too.

(DOUG *and* KENNETH *grab their roller bags and begin to exit.*)

KENNETH: Where's my bag?

DOUG: On your shoulder.

KENNETH: (Jesus.)

(KENNETH *laughs and* DOUG *gently takes his arm as they continue to exit.* KENNETH *waves at* JOHN. *He gives a small wave back.*)

(*He drinks his coffee. Looking around the airport*)

(*He touches the chocolate bar, and the* Time *magazine.*)

Scene 4

(Motel room)

(A T V plays loudly. A sitcom laugh track)

(JOHN sits on a chair, drinking a glass of water from a plastic cup.)

(He suitcase sits beside him. An airplane magazine on top)

(He chuckles with the T V.)

Scene 5

(Phoenix apartment.)

(A worn couch, a few chairs, and a dining room table.)

(PATRICIA, 30s, nervously tries to fix up the small apartment. Putting toys away in every corner)

(A large picture of Henry Owens in Marine Dress Blues sits in a frame on a shelf, next to it is a folded American flag in a glass case, and baby pictures of REGGIE with Henry and PATRICIA.)

(A knock on the door)

(PATRICIA opens the door to JOHN. And smiles)

(He holds the wrapped present, and chocolate bar.)

PATRICIA: Hi.

JOHN: Hello.
(He takes off his hat.)

(PATRICIA puts out her hand.)

PATRICIA: Patricia.

JOHN: Yes.

(JOHN shakes it, trying to manage his present, hat, and chocolate bar.)

JOHN: I think you know who I am.

PATRICIA: Yes. I do. Come on in, John.

JOHN: Thank you.

(Silence)

(PATRICIA closes the door.)

PATRICIA: Shall I take that for you?
(Silence)
Your hat?

JOHN: Oh. Yes. Yes. Please.

PATRICIA: I'll just set it over here.

JOHN: That'll work.

PATRICIA: You didn't need to bring a gift.

JOHN: Well, I thought it was appropriate.

PATRICIA: You want to put it down too? Over here?

JOHN: OK. Sure. Sure.

PATRICIA: That was thoughtful of you. And chocolate.

JOHN: I hear kids like that.

PATRICIA: Oh yeah.
(She takes the present and chocolate bar, and puts it beside his hat.)
Reggie would rot his teeth out with sweets if I let him.

(Silence)

(JOHN smooths his hair.)

PATRICIA: He's at soccer camp right now. His friend's mom is dropping him off soon.

JOHN: Oh. Okay. Fine.

PATRICIA: I thought it would work best if we had a bit of time together first anyway. Is that okay?

JOHN: Oh sure. Sure. That sounds good.
(He smiles.)

(PATRICIA *nods.*)

(*Silence*)

(JOHN *wipes his brow.*)

PATRICIA: Can I get you something to drink?

JOHN: I think I'm fine.

PATRICIA: I can make some coffee. Or tea. I have iced tea.

JOHN: I don't want to bother you.

PATRICIA: It's hot out. Are you sure?

JOHN: I don't want it to be too much trouble.

PATRICIA: It's not. Please.

(*Silence*)

JOHN: Ice tea might be nice. Yes. Thank you.

PATRICIA: I'll be right back.
(*She exits.*)

(JOHN *takes out a handkerchief and studies the room. He wipes his forehead. Sees Henry's picture on the shelf.*)

(*He slowly walks toward it.*)

(*He stops. He can only get so close.*)

PATRICIA: (*O S*) It's already sweetened. The tea. Is that Okay?

(*The flag is next to the picture.*)

(*It's almost too much.*)

(*Silence*)

PATRICIA: (*O S*) Sweetened tea, okay?

JOHN: Oh. Yes. Please. I prefer that.

PATRICIA: (*O S*) Good. Me too.

(JOHN *tries to move closer to the photo.*)

PATRICIA: *(O S)* Is it hotter here than Los Angeles?
(Silence))
John?

(JOHN stands staring at his son.)

PATRICIA: *(O S)* Is it hotter here than Los Angeles?

(Silence)

JOHN: Yes.
(He keeps staring at his son.)

PATRICIA: *(O S)* Thank goodness for air-conditioning.
(Silence)
You really can't live without it here in the desert.
(Silence)
I've been without it overseas, and it's awful.

(JOHN keeps his eyes on the photo.)

PATRICIA: *(O S)* It's miserable.

(PATRICIA finally enters with tea. Sees JOHN looking at the photo.)

PATRICIA: Have you seen that before?
(Silence)
Have you ever seen that picture?

JOHN: No.
(Silence)
No I haven't.

PATRICIA: He looks so handsome.

JOHN: Yes.

(Silence)

PATRICIA: I can get you copy if you like.

JOHN: I'd, I'd like that. Thank you.

(PATRICIA hands JOHN the tea.)

JOHN: It's a nice home you have.

PATRICIA: Oh, well. Thank you for saying that, but it's not much. It's really all I could afford. And it's close to my mother.

JOHN: I see.

PATRICIA: She helps out with Reggie.

JOHN: That's good.

PATRICIA: I'm going back to school. At night.

JOHN: You mentioned that on the phone. You like it?

PATRICIA: I do.

JOHN: What are you studying?

PATRICIA: Nursing.

JOHN: Good skill.

PATRICIA: I hope so.
(Silence)
You want to sit down?

JOHN: Sure.
(He smiles.)

*(*JOHN *and* PATRICIA *awkwardly find spots to sit on the sofa and a chair.)*

PATRICIA: I appreciate you coming.

JOHN: Well, I appreciate the invitation.
(Silence)
I'm sure it wasn't easy to make the call.

PATRICIA: No. But I'm glad you came.
(She smiles at him. Silence)
Was the flight okay?

JOHN: Oh sure. Sure.

PATRICIA: And you have a place to stay in town?

JOHN: I found a motel.

PATRICIA: Is it expensive?

JOHN: It's not too bad.

PATRICIA: I'm sorry you couldn't stay here. We just don't have the space. As you can see.

JOHN: It's no problem.
(Silence)
No problem at all.
(He pushes a smile.)
(Silence)

(More silence)

PATRICIA: I, I want to apologize for something. Before Reggie gets here.

JOHN: You don't need to apologize for anything. Really. I—

PATRICIA: No. John. Please. I want to. I, I've been feeling bad about it, and I want to say that I'm really sorry that I didn't let you come to Henry's funeral. It was selfish of me. And—

JOHN: No, no. I understand—

PATRICIA: And Gloria didn't want you to be there because she said she couldn't handle it if you were. She was freaking out about everything and Reggie was still so little and I was trying to keep it together and make plans and—

JOHN: I understand—

PATRICIA: And I've realized, lately, just how awful that must have felt.
(Silence)
And I'm sorry.

JOHN: I probably wouldn't have come anyway.

(Silence)

PATRICIA: Really?

JOHN: No.

(Silence)

PATRICIA: That's shitty.

JOHN: Yes.
(Silence)
But true.
(Silence)
I know how Gloria is, and I wouldn't have wanted
to be there and ruin it for everyone else. It was hard
enough as it is.

PATRICIA: Uh huh.

JOHN: I know I'm not the favorite person with my wife
or my son. Keeping my distance is better than bringing
up all that. The way I look at it.

(Silence)

PATRICIA: Didn't you want to make it better?

JOHN: No. Not then I didn't. No.

(Silence)

PATRICIA: I think that's selfish. I'm sorry, but—

JOHN: It is.
(Silence)
That doesn't mean I didn't, I don't think about Henry.
And feel, feel…feel…about his death. I was drunk for
a week—I've stopped drinking, by the way. I just want
you to know that.

PATRICIA: Okay.

JOHN: I've been sober for five years.

PATRICIA: Good. Good.

JOHN: My liver more than anything. Doctor's orders.
(Silence)

I probably would have kept going, if I could. But. You know.

PATRICIA: I've been clean for twelve.

JOHN: Oh. Good for you.

PATRICIA: Thank you.

JOHN: So maybe you know what I mean.

PATRICIA: It was different for me.

(Silence)

JOHN: Sure.
(Silence)
So you and Henry met in the Marines?

PATRICIA: Yes.

JOHN: Nice.

(Silence)

PATRICIA: I got out when Reggie was born.

JOHN: I see, I see.

PATRICIA: It was too hard to have both of us deployed.

JOHN: I imagine.

PATRICIA: And back then it didn't look like we would be getting out of Iraq or Afghanistan anytime soon, and I really didn't want to do another tour.

JOHN: I bet.

(Silence)

PATRICIA: You want more tea?

JOHN: I forgot about it.
(He takes a sip.)
That's good.

PATRICIA: It's a mix. Nestea.

JOHN: Tastes homemade.

PATRICIA: No.

JOHN: I like it.

(Silence)

(More silence)

PATRICIA: Since my father died, Reggie has been asking a lot of questions about you.

JOHN: Oh lord.

(This makes PATRICIA *laugh. And that surprises both* JOHN *and* PATRICIA.*)*

PATRICIA: Does that scare you?

JOHN: Yes.

*(*PATRICIA *nods.)*

JOHN: What do you tell him?

PATRICIA: Not much.

JOHN: That's the safe bet.

PATRICIA: I thought you could…you could do a better job talking about yourself than I could. And about your relationship with Henry, and—

JOHN: He's a little young for most of it.

PATRICIA: He's small but mature for his age.

JOHN: Is he?

PATRICIA: You'll see.

JOHN: Okay.

PATRICIA: He's been the man of the house since he was one. So.
(Silence)
But he's got a really good sense of humor. Really good. So don't feel like you have to, you know, give the Disney version of yourself.

JOHN: I see.

PATRICIA: Henry didn't have a chance to tell him his version of you, so I don't know, maybe that's a blessing.

JOHN: Yes. Maybe.

(Silence)

Probably.

PATRICIA: You look pretty harmless at this point.

JOHN: Old?

(PATRICIA smiles.)

JOHN: It might have made Henry happy to see me like this.

PATRICIA: You wouldn't be here if he was alive, John.

(Silence)

Is it true you beat him?

(Silence)

JOHN: Yes.

(Silence)

PATRICIA: And Gloria?

JOHN: Yes.

PATRICIA: He said you did it everyday.

(Silence)

JOHN: Just about.

PATRICIA: Why?

(Silence)

JOHN: That's not such an easy question.

PATRICIA: If I'm going to let you near my son, I need to know.

(JOHN takes out his handkerchief. He wipes his forehead.)

PATRICIA: I owe that to Henry.

(Silence)

Don't you think?

(Silence)

JOHN: I was mean. And angry.

PATRICIA: That sounds like an excuse.

JOHN: Maybe.

PATRICIA: Why take it out on them?

JOHN: Because I could.
(Silence)
I'm not proud of myself. I've paid a high price for my, my personality. I pretty much lost everything.

PATRICIA: Uh huh.

JOHN: I'm glad Gloria was smart enough to finally take Henry and go.

PATRICIA: Henry said he made her leave.

JOHN: Did he?

PATRICIA: Yes.

JOHN: Well, then he deserves the credit. For leaving.
(Silence) He was smart.

(Silence)

PATRICIA: You fucked him up.
(Silence)
Badly.
(Silence)
He deserved better.
(Silence)
But he became a good man. A great man and great Marine. He would have been a great father. He made sure he was the polar opposite of you. In every way.

JOHN: I'm proud of him for that.

PATRICIA: You could have tried to, to make amends. At some point—

JOHN: It was too late. He was killed before I had a chance. So, I guess that's my burden.
(Silence)
Maybe that's justice.

PATRICIA: You really believe that?
(Silence)
Henry said you raped someone.

JOHN: No. No. Now. No.
(Silence)
No. I never did that. He was wrong there. Who told him that?

PATRICIA: I don't know.

JOHN: Gloria, I'm sure. Damn it, no, I never raped anyone. You hear me?
(Silence)
You hear me?

PATRICIA: Yes.

(Silence)

JOHN: I robbed women, okay, but I never raped one. Not one. You have to believe me there.

PATRICIA: Okay.

JOHN: I would never do that. Never.

PATRICIA: Just beat them until they were unconscious.
(Silence)

(JOHN wipes his forehead.)

JOHN: May I use your rest room?

PATRICIA: It's down the hall there.

JOHN: Thank you.
(He stands up and slowly exits to the bathroom.)

(PATRICIA *puts her head in her hands.*)

(*She waits.*)

(*Finally,* JOHN *enters.*)

JOHN: I'm thinking maybe I should go.

PATRICIA: No. No. Please. I'm sorry. I didn't invite you here to, to—

JOHN: I think maybe this might not be a good idea.
(*He reaches for his hat.*)

(PATRICIA *stops* JOHN.)

PATRICIA: No. Please.

JOHN: I think it's best.

PATRICIA: Please.

JOHN: I think—

PATRICIA: I really didn't mean to—

JOHN: I don't want you to feel uncomfortable—

PATRICIA: I feel like I'm betraying Henry right now. By having you here.

JOHN: Uh huh.

PATRICIA: Does that make sense?

JOHN: Sure.

PATRICIA: I'm feeling guilty. I feel very very guilty right now.
(*Silence*)
The years I spent hearing about you.
(*Silence*)
The tears and…
(*Silence*)
But, but I believe people can change. Okay? I do. I know they can. My youth was nothing to brag about. Trust me.

JOHN: Well.

PATRICIA: And I invited you, right?

JOHN: Maybe you made a mistake.

PATRICIA: Do you think so?
(Silence)
Reggie really wants to meet you. He is obsessed with meeting you. He wants to meet Henry's dad, in person.
(Silence)
All the men in his life have died. All of them. His father. My brothers. My father. My uncles. You're the only one left. Who is family—

JOHN: I don't want you to feel uncomfortable with me here.

PATRICIA: I'm feeling guilty, not uncomfortable.
(Silence)
There's a difference.
(Silence)
I just, I want to know that you've changed.

JOHN: I don't know what to tell you.

(Silence)

(More silence)

JOHN: I have a bad prostate. Bad knees. A weak heart, and weak stomach.
(Silence)
I've got no more fight left in me, Patricia, if that's what you're worried about.

PATRICIA: I am, I guess.

JOHN: I haven't raised a fist in fifteen years. And I certainly wouldn't harm my grandson. I promise.
(Silence)
I promise you that.
(Silence)

I promise.

PATRICIA: Okay.

(*Silence*)

JOHN: I, I wasn't ready to be a father when Gloria and I had Henry. I really wasn't. It smothered me. The baby. I felt smothered. I hated it. If you want to know the truth. I hated all of it. It made me feel crushed against…I don't know what. Walls. Something. Normal people, maybe. Make believe. I didn't want the responsibility.

(*Silence*)

I felt like Gloria pushed me in to it. She wanted some suburban dream. Yards and barbecues and matching shirts, and I didn't care about that stuff. I was older and set in my ways.

PATRICIA: Okay.

(*Silence*)

JOHN: Not everyone is built for that kind of life. Being a father. Like that. With the baseball and, and the kid on the shoulders type thing.

PATRICIA: Okay.

JOHN: I was immature.

(*Silence*)

I wanted to drink with my friends and tear up the town and here I had this baby, this tiny baby that Gloria would push in my arms every time I came home and I didn't want it. This fragile thing. I didn't want fragile things like that in my arms, you understand. Where I had to be careful. Cautious. I didn't want something I had to love and care for. Teach things to.

(*Silence*)

I had been in and out of prison three times by the time he was born. Gloria wanted to change me. I didn't want changing. I wanted guns and women and booze. Adult things. Danger. Not pampers and sport shirts and stupid television dreams. That wasn't me. I hated that stuff. You understand? I'm not trying to make excuses, I'm trying to be honest with you. That's who I was.

(PATRICIA *brings a chair over for* JOHN.)

PATRICIA: Here. Please.

JOHN: You understand that?

PATRICIA: Yes. I do. Sit down.

JOHN: But that doesn't mean that I didn't love Henry.
(*Silence*)
Later, when I matured, I found I had a, had a great love for him. My son. And wish I could have been his father. Held him. Properly. I wish I could have—

PATRICIA: You're still his father.

JOHN: In the way he needed. And wanted.
(*Silence*)
I would have given anything to see him, later on. When he was a man. And when I was sober. Told him that I was sorry. In person. For what I had done.

PATRICIA: He wouldn't have listened.

(*Silence*)

JOHN: I never got to say good-bye.
(*Silence*)
I regret that.
(*Silence*)
There are no words for that kind of regret…just…
(*Silence*)
I don't know.
(*He finally sits.*)
(*Silence*)

PATRICIA: Can I get you more tea?

JOHN: No thank you.

(*Silence*)

JOHN: I'm really not sure this is all a good idea after all. Maybe we should wait until tomorrow.

PATRICIA: You'll go home to L A tonight if we wait until tomorrow.
(*Silence*)
Won't you?

(JOHN *takes* PATRICIA *in.*)

PATRICIA: I can feel an exit plan when it's in the air.
(*Silence*)
I had a wild youth myself. I told you.
(*Silence*)
Reggie should be here any minute.

JOHN: I think I should go.

PATRICIA: No.

(JOHN *gets up.*)

JOHN: This was a bad idea.

PATRICIA: Please. John. Please sit.

JOHN: I should go.

PATRICIA: No. Please.
(*Silence*)
Please.
(*Silence*)

JOHN: What if he doesn't like me?

PATRICIA: Why would he not like you?

JOHN: Osmosis.

(PATRICIA *smiles.*)

PATRICIA: There's really no one he doesn't like. He's very different from me and Henry.... When he was a baby he would smile at everyone and reach for them, and we were like, "where'd this kid come from?"

JOHN: There's a first for everything.

PATRICIA: Don't worry.

(*Silence*)

JOHN: This is when it's hard to be sober.

PATRICIA: Have you eaten?

JOHN: No. Not really.

PATRICIA: I'll make you a sandwich.

JOHN: No, that's okay. I don't want you to—

PATRICIA: Please.

JOHN: It's too much trouble—

PATRICIA: Reggie will be hungry when he gets home anyway. You ok with bologna?

JOHN: Sure. Okay.

PATRICIA: Mayonnaise or mustard?

JOHN: Both please.

PATRICIA: Just like Henry.

JOHN: Really?

PATRICIA: Yes.

JOHN: I guess he got something from me.

PATRICIA: He got more than that.

JOHN: I hope not.

PATRICIA: Okay, don't just sit here and feel sorry for yourself.

(*Silence*)

I really didn't want to make this a pity party. That wasn't my intention.

JOHN: Okay.

PATRICIA: I mean it.
(She just looks at him.)

(JOHN nods.)

PATRICIA: I'll be back in a minute.
(She exits.)

(JOHN stands, looks around the room.)

(They're is a small toy within reach . He picks it up. It's a military action figure.)

(He stands it on a shelf.)

(He reaches for his hat. Puts it on)

(He heads for the door. He reaches for the door knob.)

PATRICIA: *(O S)* Henry has your mouth.

(JOHN keeps his hand on the door knob.)

(He's surrounded by baby pictures. Child paintings. That folded flag, in a glass case)

(He opens the door, quietly.)

PATRICIA: *(O S)* John?
(Silence)
John?
(Silence)

JOHN: Yes?

PATRICIA: *(O S)* I said, Henry had your mouth.

JOHN: Oh?

PATRICIA: *(O S)* And your build.

(Silence)

JOHN: Yeah?

*(The folded flag in a glass case—*JOHN *can't take his eyes off it. The flag that was draped over Henry's coffin.)*

PATRICIA: *(O S)* Gloria always wants to take credit for Henry's looks, but I see that he didn't get them from her.

(Silence)

JOHN: She was very beautiful when she was young.

PATRICIA: *(O S)* That's what she says.

JOHN: It's true.

(Silence)

PATRICIA: *(O S)* We don't get along that great. Actually.

JOHN: That doesn't surprise me.

PATRICIA: *(O S)* Why?

JOHN: You're pretty. She feels threatened.

(Silence)

PATRICIA: *(O S)* I never considered that.

JOHN: Consider it. She was jealous of every woman I ever looked at.

PATRICIA: *(O S)* I hear you did more than look at them.

JOHN: Well. I'm human.

(Sounds of water and closing fridges, etc)

PATRICIA: *(O S)* You want chips with your sandwich? *(Silence)* Chips, John?

JOHN: No thank you.

PATRICIA: *(O S)* You're sure?

JOHN: Yes.
(He slowly closes the door.)
(And places his head against it.)
(He stands unsure what to do next.)

(PATRICIA *finally enters with a sandwich on a plate, and chips. She sets it down on the table.*)

PATRICIA: I gave you chips.

JOHN: Oh. Okay.

PATRICIA: I think you're just being polite.

(*Silence*)

(PATRICIA *sees the hat on* JOHN's *head. He takes it off.*)

JOHN: I want you to know I'm no monster.

PATRICIA: I know you do. But if you're hungry, you should eat.

(JOHN *doesn't move.*)

JOHN: I'm—

PATRICIA: I know.
(*Silence*)
Are you okay?

JOHN: Yes.

PATRICIA: You want some help?

JOHN: No.

PATRICIA: Come sit down.

(JOHN *walks over to the table.*)

(PATRICIA *takes his hat.*)

JOHN: Aren't you going to eat?

PATRICIA: I'm on a diet.

JOHN: Why?

PATRICIA: *Why?* So I can fit in my goddamn jeans.

(*Silence*)

JOHN: You look fine.

PATRICIA: Tell that to my mirror.
(*Silence*)

I want to start dating again.

JOHN: Oh?

PATRICIA: I can't talk to Gloria about it. She cries every time.

JOHN: That's Gloria.

PATRICIA: It's been six years, for Christ's sake. I think it's about time I try and meet someone. Before I'm too old and no one wants me. I can't mourn forever.
(*She sits down beside him at the table.*)

(*Silence*)

JOHN: This table looks familiar.

PATRICIA: Gloria gave it to us.

JOHN: I think it was a wedding gift from her parents.

PATRICIA: That's what she said.

JOHN: I never liked it.

PATRICIA: I don't either. But, she wanted us to have it. And beats buying a new one.

JOHN: She used to sit right there and stare daggers at me. And I was such a son-of-a-bitch, and drunk, I'd just stare back at her, and keep eating bite by bite, as slow as I could, until she'd start crying and left the room.

PATRICIA: Huh.

JOHN: That's pretty much how it went. For seven years.

PATRICIA: Why'd you stick around?

JOHN: It was a place to sleep at night. Money. Her parents bought the house. The car. The—

PATRICIA: Were her parents wealthy?

JOHN: No. Controlling.
(*He eats.*)

JOHN: They all wanted to turn me around.
(Silence)
Jail was easier for me than that house.

(Silence)

(PATRICIA *looks around the apartment.*)

PATRICIA: I'd like to get out of here, but it will be awhile. Everything's so damn expensive. We got some money from the government when Henry died, but I'm saving that for Reggie's college. You should see what people pay for university now.

JOHN: I hear.

PATRICIA: Night school's not cheap, but if Reggie wants to go to Yale or something fancy like that, we have to save that money.

JOHN: Is that what he wants?

PATRICIA: He's seven, so it changes daily. But he's smart, so he if he works hard, he might have some options. I'm not letting him go in to the military.

JOHN: No?

(Silence)

PATRICIA: They aren't taking my son too.
(Silence)
(She pushes a smile.)

(Silence)

JOHN: Does Reggie play baseball?

PATRICIA: No. Why?

JOHN: I bought him a baseball mitt.
(He motions to the present.)
I thought he might like that.

PATRICIA: From you, he'll love it.

JOHN: You think?

PATRICIA: Yes.

JOHN: Does he have one?

PATRICIA: Yes.

JOHN: Really? Damn it.

PATRICIA: But he doesn't have one from you.

JOHN: I can take it back.

PATRICIA: No, no. Don't.

JOHN: Is there something he'd rather have?

PATRICIA: No.

(Silence)

JOHN: I feel silly giving him something he already has. Seems like a waste.

PATRICIA: If you gave him a rubber chicken, he'd love it. It doesn't matter what—

JOHN: Does he have a rubber chicken?

PATRICIA: No.

JOHN: Then maybe I should switch the mitt.

PATRICIA: That's not my point.

JOHN: I was just thinking, it would be nice if he had, you know, something special to remember me by. A baseball mitt seemed like something he could use and—

PATRICIA: Do me a favor?

JOHN: What?

PATRICIA: Don't think about giving Reggie "something special to remember you by". Please.
(Silence)
That's all he's got of his father. Objects to remember him by.
(Silence)

Just stay. Spend time with him. Let him remember that.
(Silence)
The poor kid is surrounded by ghosts.
(Silence)
Give him someone living.

(Silence)

JOHN: He ever ask about his dad?

PATRICIA: Sometimes. Yes. It goes in phases.

JOHN: What do you tell him?

PATRICIA: The truth.

JOHN: You tell him how he died?

PATRICIA: Yes.

JOHN: The details?

(Silence)

PATRICIA: Most of them.

JOHN: Jesus.

PATRICIA: Listen, I'm not a fairy tale type person.
(Silence)
Henry's his father. He should know what happened to
him, and how and why. And that his father was killed
doing something he really believed in.
(Silence)
It doesn't matter what other people believe.
(Silence)
I don't talk to him about that.

(Silence)

JOHN: You angry?

PATRICIA: No. No. Just…just a little…I don't know.
(Silence)
Lost. Maybe.
(Silence)

I don't know anymore.
(*She checks her watch.*)
I want you to know that sometimes, sometimes Reggie gets shy. When he gets overwhelmed, he can get shy. And he might act weird. At first. He loves everyone, but there are times he gets overwhelmed and shy and has to run to his room. So I just don't want you to talk it personally.

JOHN: Okay.

PATRICIA: He's seven. I mean, c'mon…he's not rational sometimes.
(*Silence*)
It doesn't mean he doesn't like you.
(*Silence*)
Okay?
(*Silence*)
And don't start feeling sorry for yourself. He doesn't need that crap, okay?

JOHN: Okay.
(*Silence*)
Thanks for the tip.

PATRICIA: I don't want you to run out too. I can't handle two crazy Owens boys at once.

JOHN: I'll try to control myself.

PATRICIA: I know you have a habit. Of running.
(*Silence*)
I need you to grow up. Right now.

(JOHN *just looks at* PATRICIA.)

PATRICIA: I'm serious.
(*Silence*)
And finish your sandwich.

(JOHN *begins to eat.*)

JOHN: You're a little bossy. Anyone ever mention that to you?

PATRICIA: Yes. Often.

JOHN: I've been meeting a lot of bossy people lately.

PATRICIA: Yeah?

JOHN: Seems so. Yes.

PATRICIA: What's the alternative?

JOHN: I don't know.

PATRICIA: Exactly.

(Silence)

JOHN: You must have been a good Marine.

PATRICIA: I was fantastic.

JOHN: Reggie is in good hands then.

(Silence)

PATRICIA: I hope so.
(Silence)
I'm what he's got.
(Silence)
Keep eating.

(JOHN *picks up his sandwich when the door opens, and in walks* REGGIE. *A small seven year old in soccer clothes.)*

(JOHN *stands.)*

REGGIE: Mom?
(He stops when he sees JOHN.*)*

PATRICIA: Hi sweetheart. Look who's here. You're Grandpa John.

(JOHN *wipes his hands on his napkin.)*

(*He slowly stands and walks toward* REGGIE.*)*

JOHN: Well. Hello.

(He puts out his hand, realizing he's too tall above the boy.)

(JOHN bends down on one knee, [this is not easy for him, with his bad knees] to get down on REGGIE's level.)

(He puts out his hand.)

JOHN: Reggie.

(REGGIE looks at JOHN and looks at his hand. Then looks at PATRICIA.)

(REGGIE looks at JOHN again. His hand in front of him)

JOHN: I'm very happy to meet you—

(REGGIE jumps in JOHN's arms, hugging him.)

(JOHN puts his arms around his grandson.)

(He hugs him tightly.)

(He hugs him, properly.)

Scene 6

(The city sidewalk, Los Angeles)

(The overflowing shopping cart sits off by itself. There are bunches of flowers in cellophane leaning up against the cart. Candles are set up as a small alter.)

(JOHN walks slowly on stage and sees the cart. He carries the usual fruit in his hand, along with an airline flight magazine.)

(He approaches the cart. Takes it in)

(He sets the fruit at the alter, next to the candles. And the souvenir from the flight. He puts a small Marine action figure, from REGGIE, beside it.)

(He takes it all in.)

JOHN: Good bye.

END OF PLAY